The Life of
Sacagawea

By Maria Nelson

 Gareth Stevens
Publishing

Please visit our website, www.garethstevens.com. For a free color catalog of all our high-quality books, call toll free 1-800-542-2595 or fax 1-877-542-2596.

Library of Congress Cataloging-in-Publication Data

Nelson, Maria.
The life of Sacagawea / Maria Nelson.
    p. cm. — (Famous lives)
Includes bibliographical references and index.
ISBN 978-1-4339-6359-9 (pbk.)
ISBN 978-1-4339-6360-5 (6-pack)
ISBN 978-1-4339-6357-5 (library binding)
1. Sacagawea—Juvenile literature. 2. Shoshoni women—Biography—Juvenile literature. 3. Shoshoni Indians—Biography—Juvenile literature. 4. Lewis and Clark Expedition (1804-1806)—Juvenile literature. I. Title.
F592.7.S123N44 2012
978.04'9745740092—dc23
[B]
                                        2011035145

First Edition

Published in 2012 by
Gareth Stevens Publishing
111 East 14th Street, Suite 349
New York, NY 10003

Copyright © 2012 Gareth Stevens Publishing

Designer: Daniel Hosek
Editor: Kristen Rajczak

Photo credits: Cover, pp. 1, 7 Shutterstock.com; pp. 5, 11, 13 MPI/Getty Images; p. 9 Gamma-Rapho/ Getty Images; p. 15 SuperStock/Getty Images; p. 17 © The Granger Collection; p. 19 Marilyn Angel Wynn/Nativestock/Getty Images; p. 21 Mike Theiler/Getty Images.

Printed in the United States of America

CPSIA compliance information: Batch #CW12GS: For further information contact Gareth Stevens, New York, New York at 1-800-542-2595.

Contents

Boldface words appear in the glossary.

Many Stories

Sacagawea is famous for helping Meriwether Lewis and William Clark **explore** the western United States. However, many other facts about her life are uncertain.

5

Early Life

Sacagawea was born around 1788. Her father was a Shoshone Indian chief. When Sacagawea was about 12 years old, Hidatsu Indians **raided** her home. They took her away with them.

7

Going West

Sacagawea married a fur trader named Toussaint Charbonneau in 1804. He was hired to **interpret** for explorers Lewis and Clark. They were studying the land in the American West.

Clark

Lewis

9

Sacagawea was chosen to travel with Lewis and Clark, too. She could speak to the Shoshone Indians for them.

A Helpful Guide

Sacagawea had a baby son just before leaving with the explorers in 1805. Together, they were very helpful. A woman and baby showed the Native Americans they met that the explorers came in peace.

13

Sacagawea's most important task on the journey was helping the explorers cross the Rocky Mountains. She got them horses and a guide from her brother. He was the chief of a nearby Shoshone **tribe**.

Sacagawea knew a great deal about the land the group traveled through. She found plants that could be eaten. She also made clothing.

The Mystery

After traveling with Lewis and Clark, it is believed that Sacagawea had a daughter. Some people say Sacagawea died soon after that, around 1812. Others believe she returned to her tribe and lived until 1884.

SACAJAWEA
DIED·APRIL·9·1884
A·GUIDE·WITH·THE
LEWIS·AND·CLARK
EXPEDITION
1805 — 1806
IDENTIFIED·1907·BY
REV·J·ROBERTS
WHO·OFFICIATED·AT
HER·BURIAL

19

Remembering Sacagawea

There are many places around the United States that honor Sacagawea. Mountains are named for her. In 2000, the US **Mint** put her picture on the dollar coin!

Timeline

1788 — Sacagawea is born.

1804 — Sacagawea marries Toussaint Charbonneau.

1805 — Sacagawea travels with Lewis and Clark.

1812 or **1884** — Sacagawea dies.

2000 — The Sacagawea dollar coin comes out.

Glossary

explore: to search in order to find out new things

interpret: to explain the meaning of another language

mint: a place where coins are made

raid: a surprise battle

tribe: a group of people who live, work, and move about together

For More Information

Books

Berne, Emma Carlson. *Sacagawea: Crossing the Continent with Lewis & Clark*. New York, NY: Sterling, 2010.

Crosby, Michael T. *Sacagawea: Shoshone Explorer*. Stockton, NJ: OTTN Publishing, 2008.

Websites

Go West Across America with Lewis & Clark!
www.nationalgeographic.com/west/
Learn more about the famous journey and play a game.

The Shoshone
www.ilovehistory.utah.gov/people/first_peoples/tribes/
shoshone.html
Read about Sacagawea's tribe and where they live today.

Index